MERCY OTIS WARREN

The Woman Who Wrote for Others

U.S. REVOLUTIONARY PERIOD | BIOGRAPHY 4TH GRADE | CHILDREN'S BIOGRAPHIES

First Edition, 2020

Published in the United States by Speedy Publishing LLC, 40 E Main Street, Newark, Delaware 19711 USA.

© 2020 Dissected Lives Books, an imprint of Speedy Publishing LLC

Dissected Lives Books are available at special discounts when purchased in bulk for industrial and sales-promotional use. For details contact our Special Sales Team at Speedy Publishing LLC, 40 E Main Street, Newark, Delaware 19711 USA. Telephone (888) 248-4521 Fax: (210) 519-4043.

10 9 8 7 6 * 5 4 3 2 1

Print Edition: 9781541950818
Digital Edition: 9781541952614

See the world in pictures. Build your knowledge in style.
www.speedypublishing.com

TABLE OF CONTENTS

In this book, we're going to talk about the life of Mercy Otis Warren and her influence during the Revolutionary War, so let's get right to it!

Who Was Mercy Otis Warren?

MERCY OTIS WARREN

orn in Barnstable, Massachusetts on the 25th of September 1728, Mercy Otis Warren became an influential writer during the American Revolution. The political leaders of the day conferred with her about their future plans for the fledgling country. Through her many writings, she promoted the idea of democracy, a type of government run by the majority vote of its citizens. At the time, many of the colonists thought that such a government would never be possible. After all, before the Revolution, the colonies were ruled by Great Britain and the monarchy had an iron fist.

In addition to promoting democracy, Mercy also was influential in the fight for women's rights. As the colonies began to protest Great Britain and the colonial American leaders began to discuss creating a new nation, she became an important figure. During her lifetime she provided historical details and relevant commentary on the initial history of the United States.

A MEETING OF COLONISTS PROTESTING BRITISH
TREATMENT BEFORE THE AMERICAN REVOLUTION.

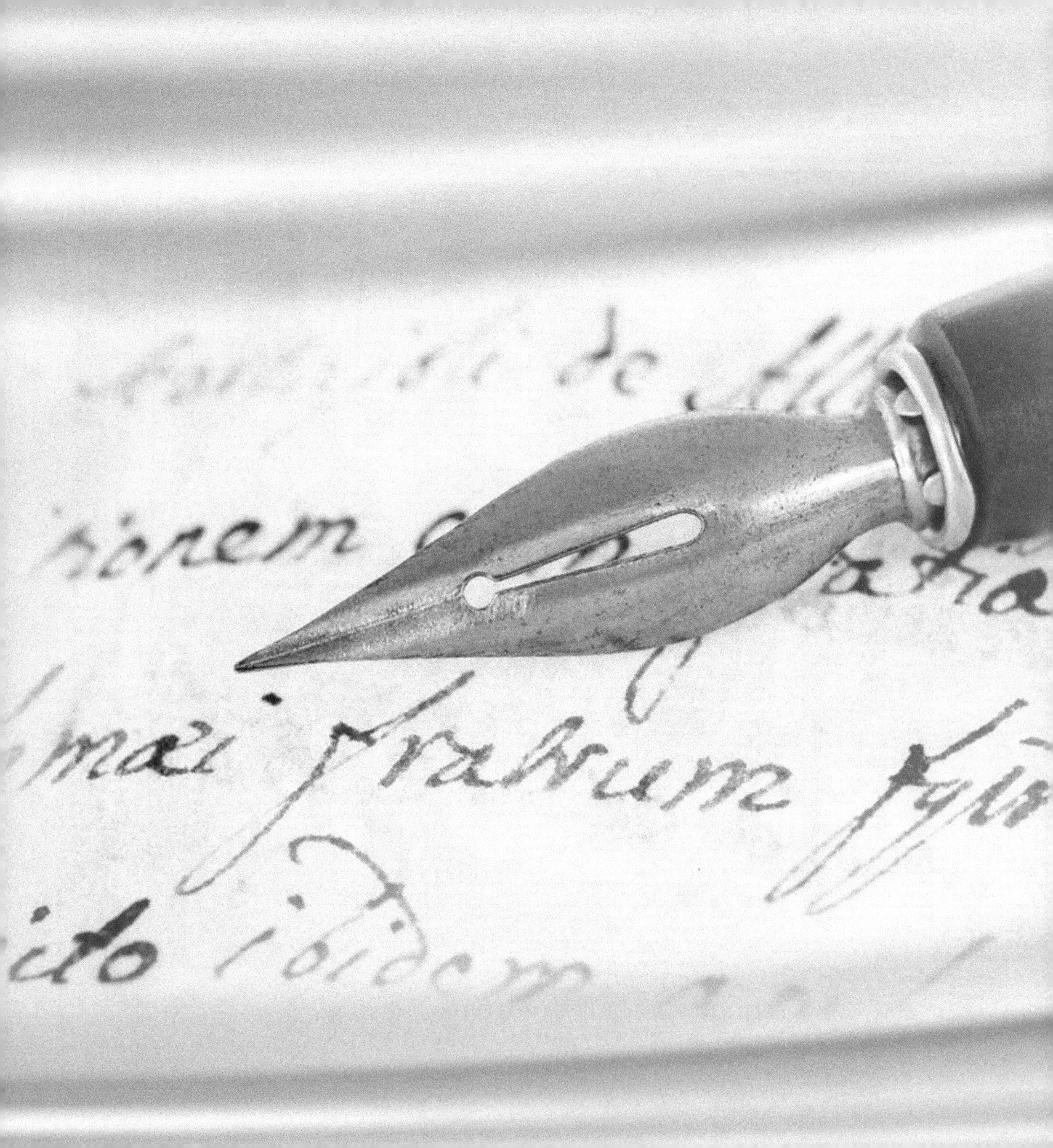

MERCY'S EARLY YEARS

Mercy's parents, Mary Allyne Otis and Colonel James Otis, eventually had thirteen children. Mercy was their third child and she was their first girl. Mercy's ancestors had arrived at Plymouth on the Mayflower ship in 1620 so they were some of the first colonists.

LANDING PARTY FROM THE "MAYFLOWER"
ARRIVING AT PLYMOUTH, 1620.

COLONEL JAMES OTIS

JAMES OTIS, JR.

As an officer in the militia and a successful farmer, her father provided a good life for his family. Her father eventually became an influential judge in their county. Mercy had a close relationship with James, her eldest brother, who was nicknamed Jemmy.

Mercy's parents made sure that their sons were ready to attend college, but, as was the case in those days, they didn't expect to send their daughters. But, Mercy had a desire to learn so she would make an effort to listen to the lessons her older brothers were receiving in literature as well as history. Their uncle was often their tutor and Mercy spent many happy hours selecting and reading books from his library.

MERCY'S UNCLE WAS HER TUTOR.

MERCY WAS ALLOWED TO TAKE PART IN DEBATES AND CONVERSATIONS WITH HER BROTHER AND FATHER.

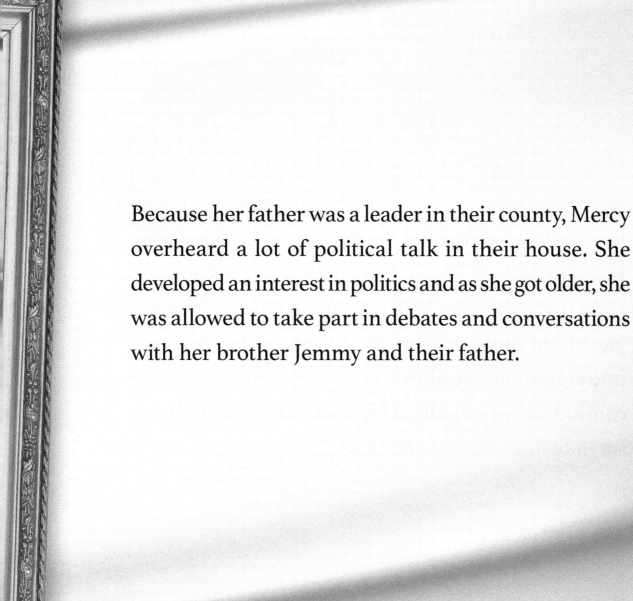

Because her father was a leader in their county, Mercy overheard a lot of political talk in their house. She developed an interest in politics and as she got older, she was allowed to take part in debates and conversations with her brother Jemmy and their father.

In 1743, Jemmy attended and received a degree from Harvard College. Today, Harvard College is known as Harvard University. When Jemmy graduated, Mercy journeyed there to sit in on the ceremony. After his undergraduate studies, Jemmy returned home to continue his studies for a graduate degree and Mercy sat in on his tutoring once more.

HARVARD UNIVERSITY, CAMBRIDGE, MASSACHUSETTS

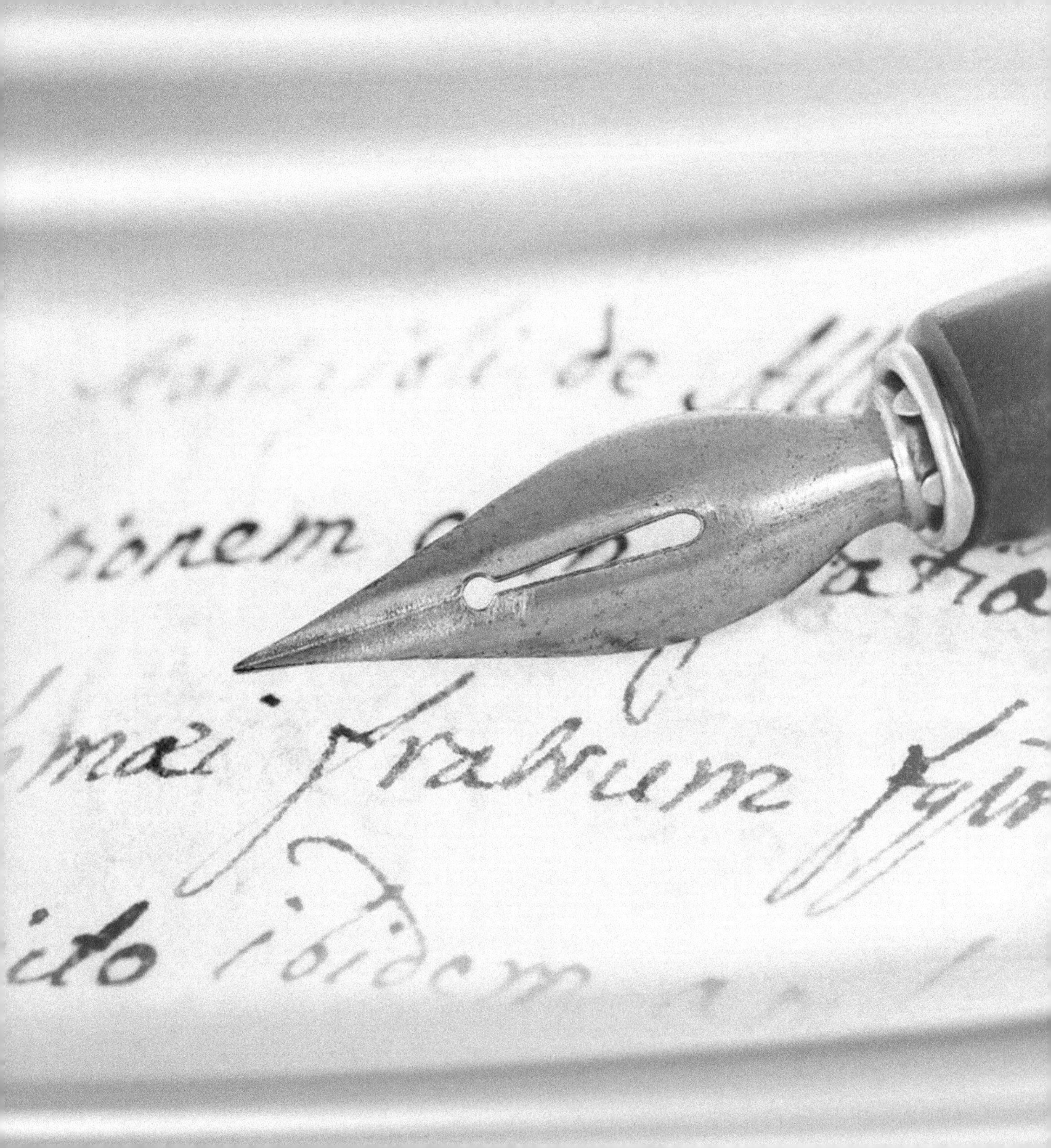

MERCY'S MARRIAGE

In November of 1754, Mercy Otis and James Warren were married. Mercy's husband was very accomplished. Like her brother, he was a Harvard graduate. He was a merchant as well as a farmer. The two had met through their family connections. In fact, they shared a great-great-grandfather, who had come to America on the Mayflower. Their 50-year marriage became a very strong one based on love as well as mutual admiration and respect.

JAMES WARREN

THE WINSLOW-WARREN HOUSE AT THE CORNER OF NORTH AND MAIN STREETS IN PLYMOUTH WAS THE LONGTIME HOME OF MERCY OTIS WARREN, HER HUSBAND JAMES WARREN, AND THEIR FIVE SONS.

Mercy and James lived at his family's home in Plymouth, not far from Mercy's family. Mercy took care of James's sick father as James began to pursue a career in the law. Three years after Mercy and James married, James's father passed away and he inherited the estate. One of the assets was a house named Winslow House. It was in a central location in Plymouth, and the couple moved there to get ready for their first baby. They named their first son, James Junior, after his father. Mercy would give birth to four more sons. They named their second son, Winslow after their house. Next there was Charles, then Henry, and last of all George who was born in 1766, when Mercy was 38 years old.

THE
PATRIOTS

As her sons grew up and her father, her brother, and her husband became more involved in politics, Mercy found herself at the heart of it all. They were all Patriots, which meant that they wanted the colonies to become independent of Great Britain.

AN ICONIC IMAGE RELATING TO THE PATRIOTIC SENTIMENT SURROUNDING THE AMERICAN REVOLUTIONARY WAR.

VOTE WHIG

WHIGS to the RESCUE!

EY COULDN'T POSSIBLY BE WORSE

In 1765, her husband James won a seat as a Representative of the state of Massachusetts. Her brother Jemmy was a leader in the Whig political party, which was against Great Britain keeping a stronghold on the colonies.

31

As the tension between the colonies and Great Britain began to increase, their home became a meeting place for the great thinkers and political leaders of the day, such as George Washington and John Adams as well as Alexander Hamilton and Samuel Adams, all of whom became Founding Fathers of the new country.

GEORGE WASHINGTON

ALEXANDER HAMILTON

JOHN ADAMS

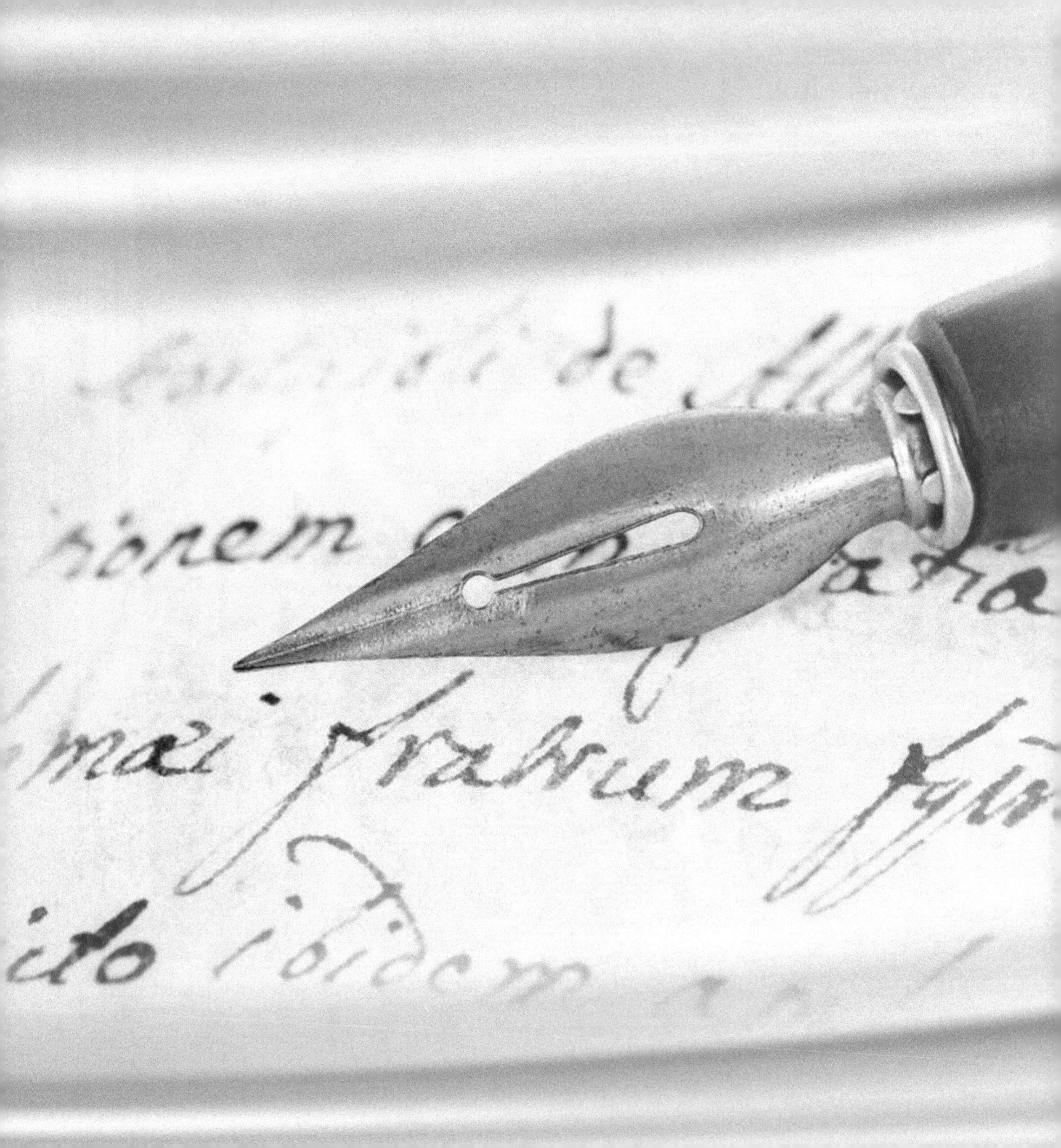

MERCY
BEGINS TO
WRITE

An attorney with a huge network of contacts, Mercy's brother Jemmy was one of the first American leaders to challenge the British monarchy. In 1761, he gave a speech, which later became famous due to his phrase claiming that there shouldn't be taxation without representation. But, Jemmy had one downfall. He had a terrible temper and he got into a fight. A profound blow to the head left him permanently injured. Mercy wanted to carry on his work, but at that time women couldn't hold political office. So, she decided that the best way she could contribute would be to use her writing to further the cause of America's independence.

BRONZE SCULPTURE OF JAMES OTIS JR. IN FRONT OF THE BARNSTABLE COUNTY COURTHOUSE, MASSACHUSETTS

SAMUEL ADAMS

In 1772, Mercy and her husband James hosted a very important meeting at their home. Samuel Adams as well as other revolutionary figures were in attendance. The idea was floated that there should be committees that would maintain correspondence about the political climate. These organized groups would share their thoughts on how the colonies could move toward independence.

Mercy started to write plays about politics. She didn't expect that these plays would be performed. Instead, she hoped that people would read her plays and come to understand the philosophy and mindset of the Patriots. She felt strongly that instead of being governed by an official appointed by the British monarchy that the colonies would benefit by being governed by representatives who were elected to their positions by the citizens.

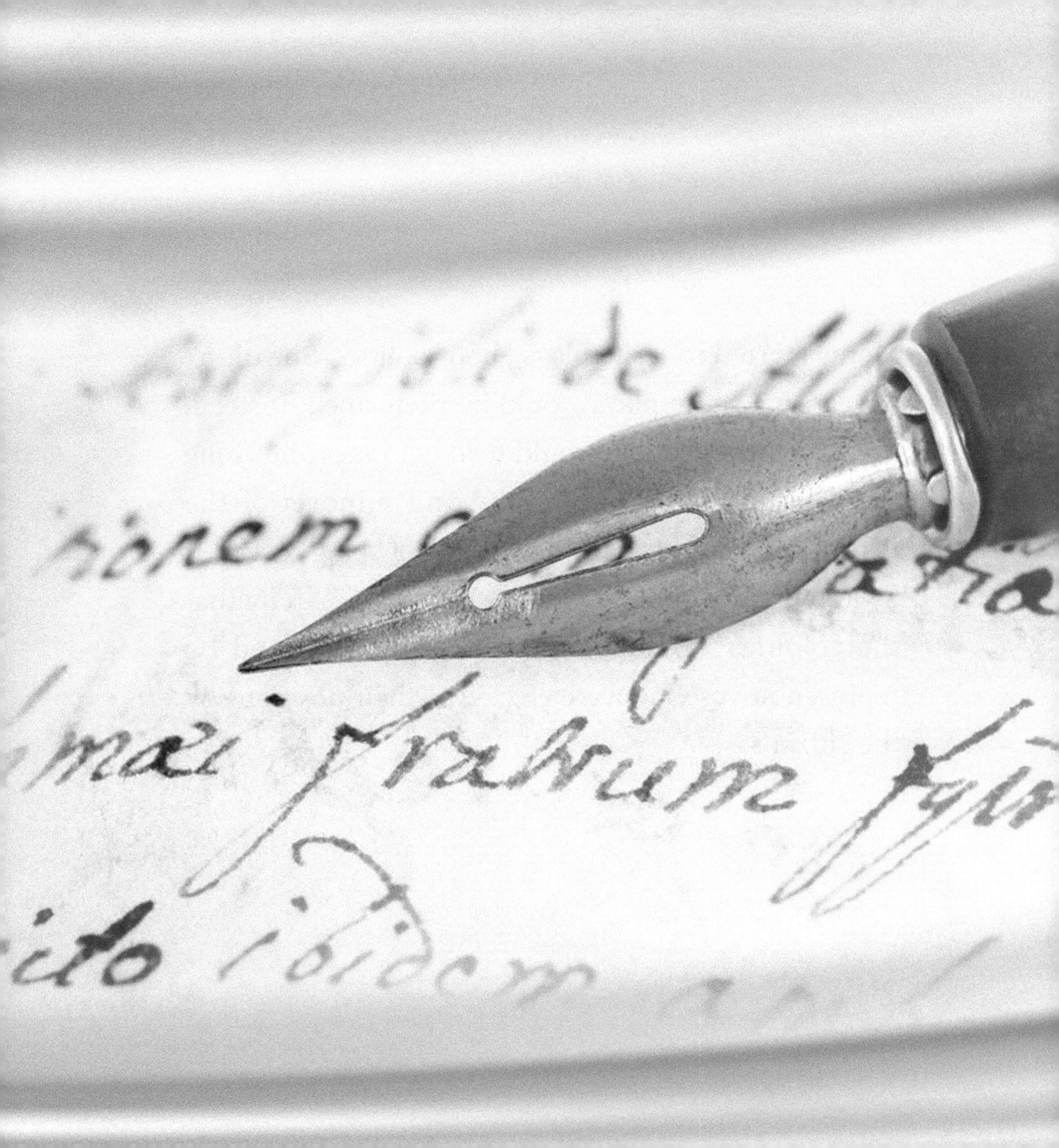

Mercy's First Published Work

In 1765, Mercy wrote poetry to share among family and friends. She penned a poem about liberty for the state of Massachusetts and it became the lyrics for a well-known and popular song.

In 1772, at the age of 44, Mercy had her first play published. It was called *The Adulateur*. The play was a satire, which means that it used biting humor in order to criticize.

THE
Adulateur.

ACT I. SCENE I.

A street in SERVIA.

Enter BRUTUS *and* CASSIUS.

BRUTUS.

IS this the once fam'd miſtreſs of the north ?
The ſweet retreat of freedom ? dearly pur-
    chas'd !
A clime matur'd with blood ; from whoſe
    rich ſoil,
Has ſprung a glorious harveſt.—Oh ! my friend,
The change how drear ! the ſullen ghoſt of bondage,
Stalks full in view—already with her pinions,
She ſhades the affrighted land—th' inſulting ſoldi-
    ers,
Tread down our choiceſt rights ; while hoodwink'd
    juſtice
Drops her ſcales, and totters from her baſis.
Thus torn with nameleſs wounds, my bleeding
    country
Demands a tear—that tear I'll ſ

Caſſius. Oh !

THOMAS HUTCHINSON

In the play, the Massachusetts governor, Thomas Hutchinson, was presented as the villain of the story. His code name was Rapatio. In the story, he's eager to cause destruction to the colony, whereas the hero, Brutus, rallies the people to resist with his passionate oration. It was clear that Mercy modeled the hero after her brother, Jemmy.

Excerpts from the play were published in a newspaper called the *Massachusetts Spy*. The *Adulateur* was published anonymously, which means that her name wasn't credited. During that time period, it was considered "inappropriate" for a woman to be a playwright. A year after excerpts were released, the play was issued as a booklet with additional text from another writer.

MASTHEAD OF THE MASSACHUSETTS SPY, A NEWSPAPER FOUNDED BY ISAIAH THOMAS IN 1771 AND PUBLISHED IN BOSTON, MASSACHUSETTS.

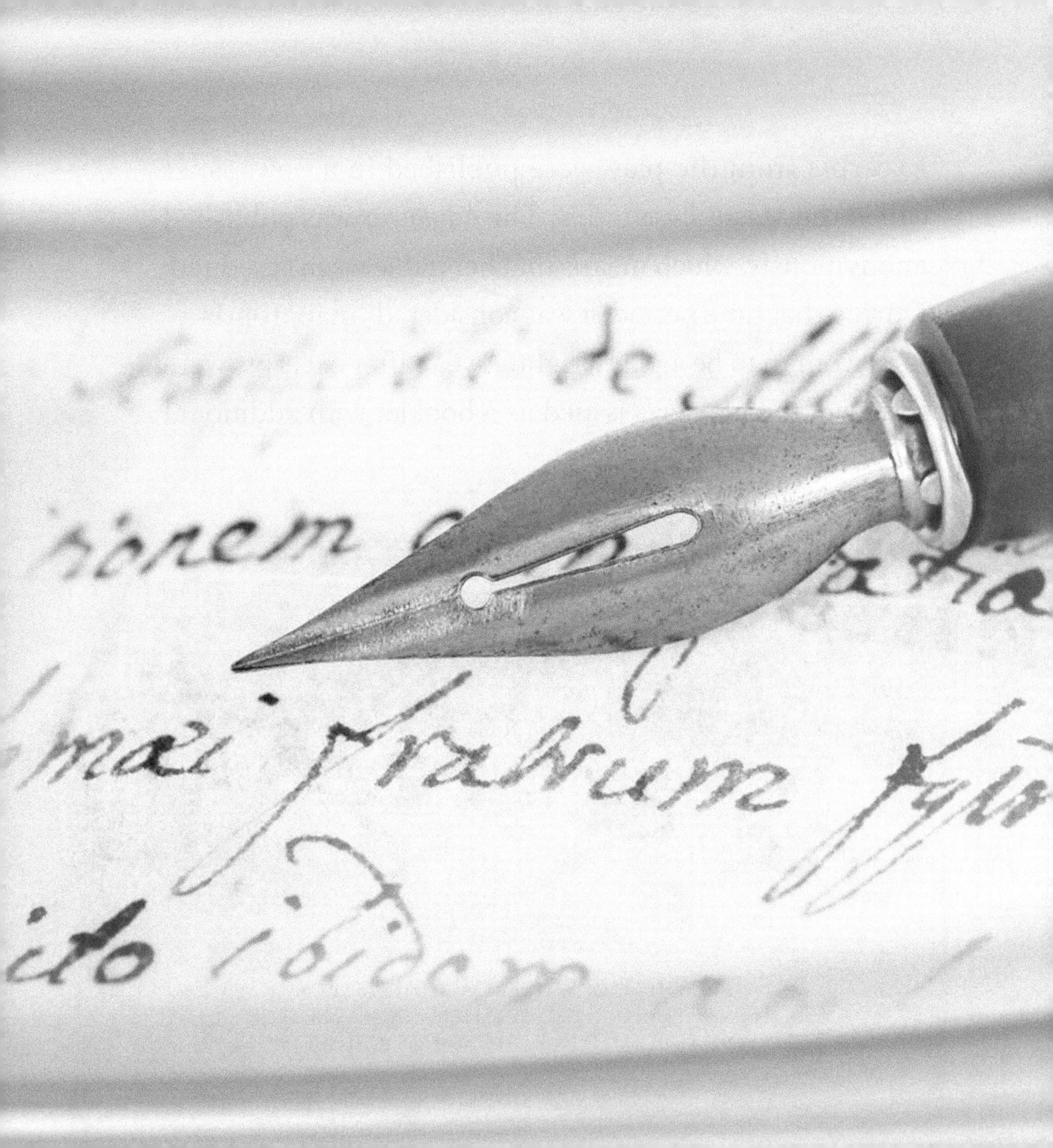

MERCY
CONTINUES
TO WRITE

ercy had been penning poems and patriotic letters since the middle of the 1700s, but until the publication of *The Adulateur* she had only shared her work with her family members and her friends. After its publication, her work became known by a much larger audience and began to have an influence on others.

BRONZE SCULPTURE OF MERCY OTIS WARREN IN FRONT OF
THE BARNSTABLE COUNTY COURTHOUSE, MASSACHUSETTS

MERCY USED CODES FOR THE POLITICAL LEADERS, BUT IT WAS OBVIOUS WHOM THE CHARACTERS WERE PORTRAYING.

Next, Mercy wrote a play in three acts called *The Defeat*. Her earlier character, Rapatio, was a villain in this play as well. She used codes for the political leaders, but it was obvious whom the characters were portraying. Her satirical attacks on the British made them appear a lot less in control, therefore giving the Patriots hope that they might be successful in their cause of independence for America.

The year that the American Revolution started, 1775, Mercy's play *The Group* was released. Since Thomas Hutchinson had returned to Europe and her Rapatio character was based on him, she added some different villains. She also began to champion women's rights since she stated that women should be allowed to leave husbands who were abusing them. Later in 1775, her new play was published in booklet form and distributed in New York as well as Philadelphia and Boston. Her work was now reaching a wide audience.

GROUP,

A

FARCE:

As lately Acted, and to be Re-acted, to the Wonder
of all superior Intelligences;

NIGH HEAD QUARTERS, AT

AMBOYNE.

IN TWO ACTS.

JAMAICA, Printed;

PHILADELPHIA, Re-printed;

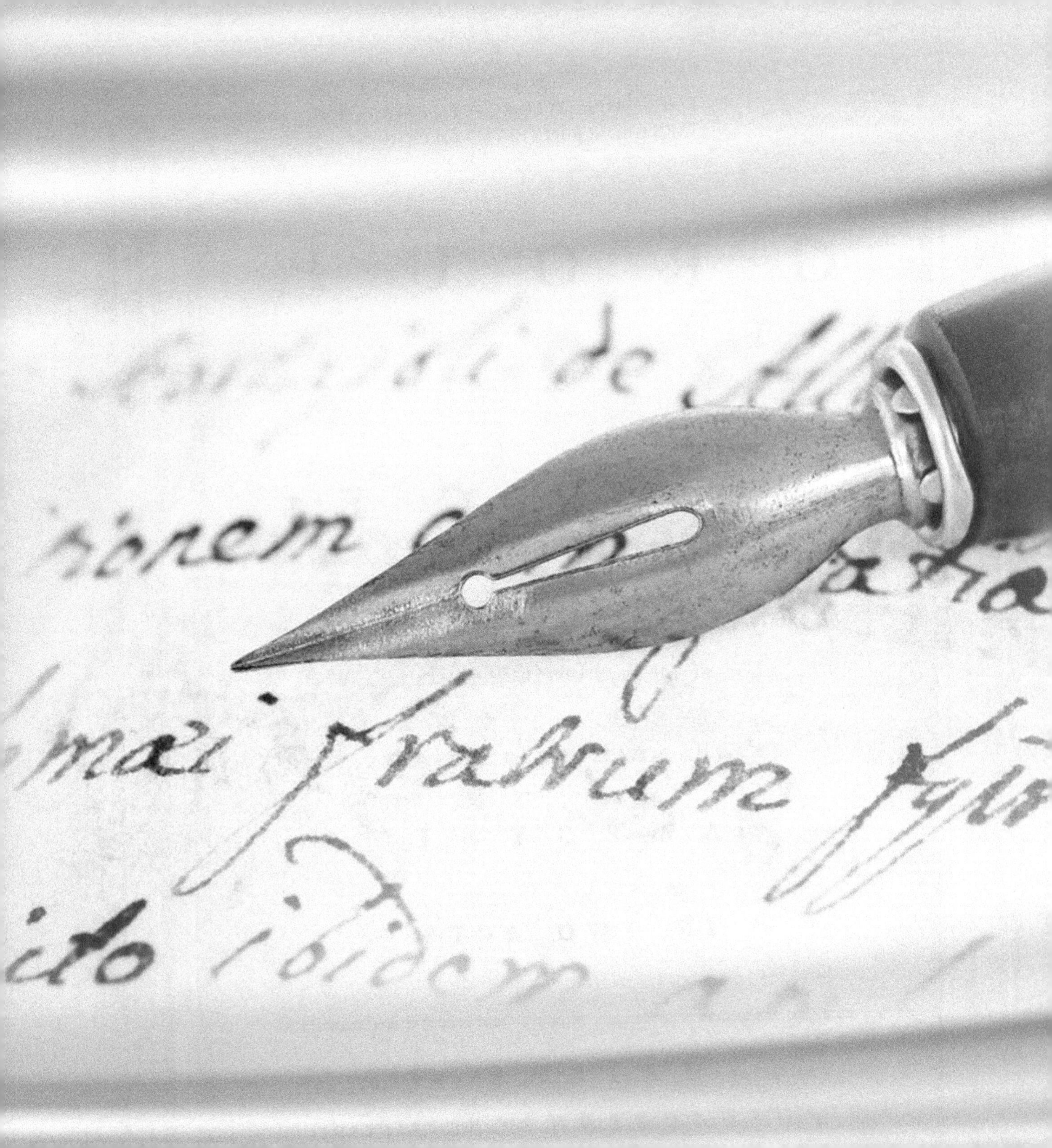
de
fratrum

Mercy's Friendship with Abigail Adams

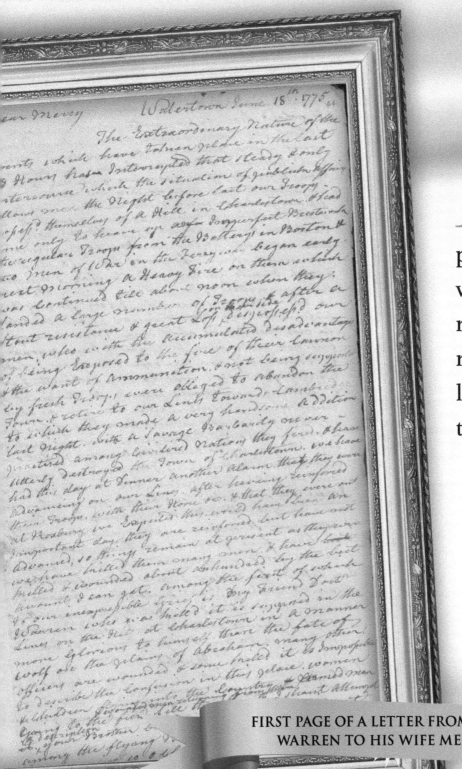

As the Revolution progressed, Mercy continued to write prose and began to include women characters in her new work. Her husband, now a general, was gone for long stretches of time and they wrote to each other.

Mercy and her husband began a close friendship with future United States President John Adams and Abigail Adams, his wife. Even though Mercy was much older than Abigail, the two women developed a close bond and emotionally supported each other during the difficult war years.

ABIGAIL ADAMS

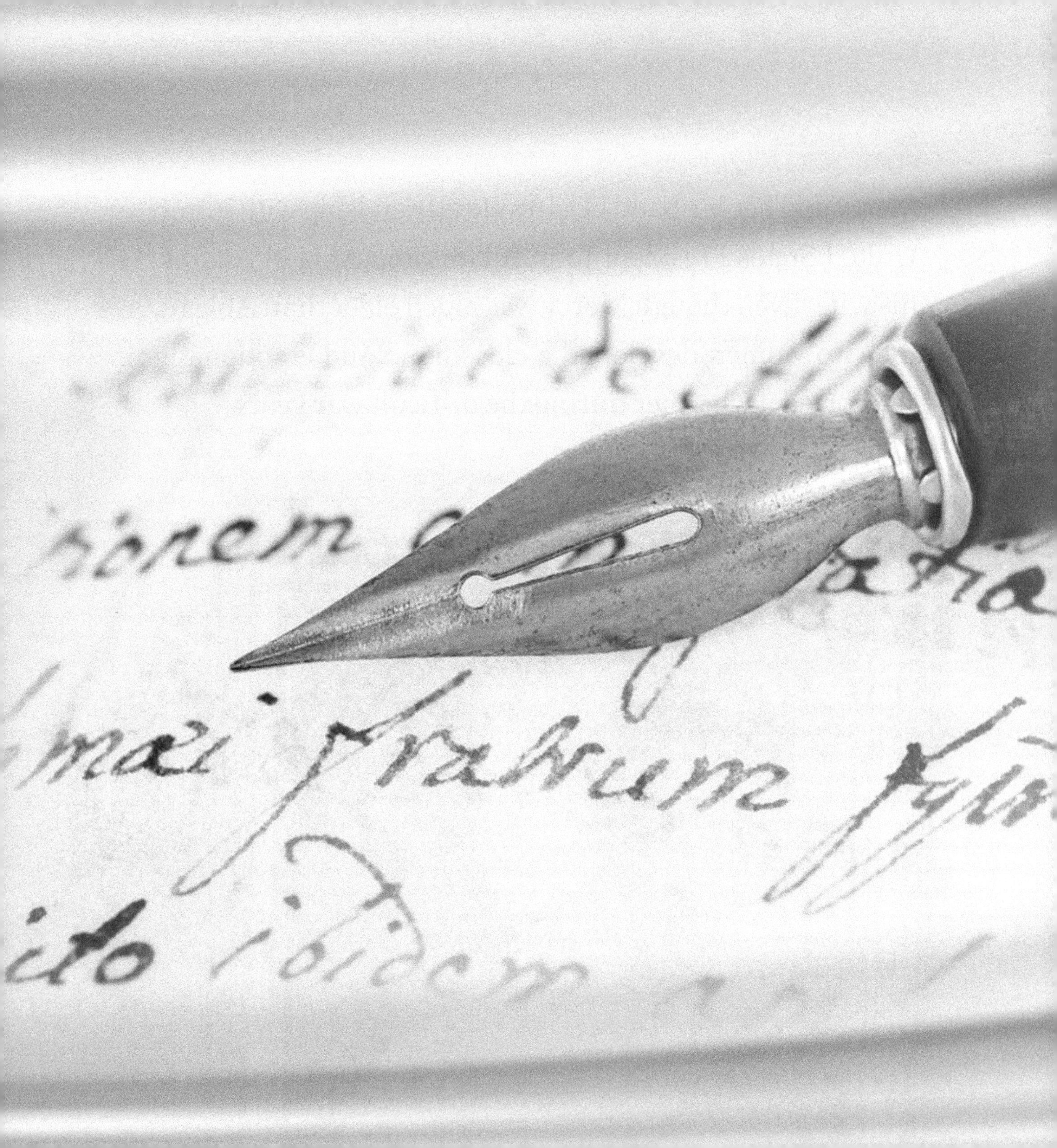

A New
Nation

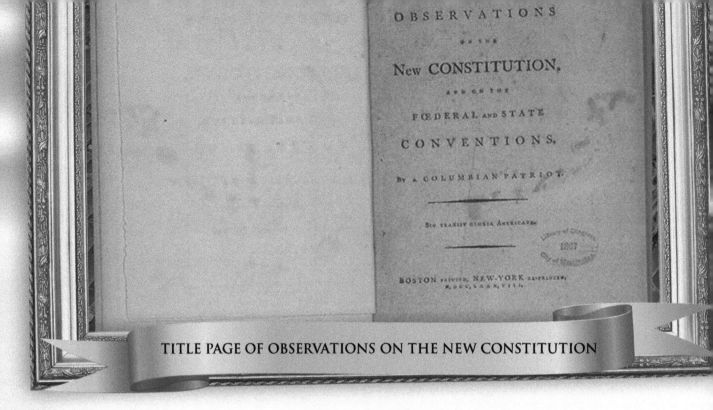

OBSERVATIONS

ON THE

New CONSTITUTION,

AND ON THE

FŒDERAL AND STATE

CONVENTIONS,

BY A COLUMBIAN PATRIOT.

SIC TRANSIT GLORIA AMERICANA

BOSTON PRINTED, NEW-YORK REPRINTED,
M,DCC,LXXXVIII.

TITLE PAGE OF OBSERVATIONS ON THE NEW CONSTITUTION

After the colonies were victorious against Britain, and the United States of America was formed, Mercy continued to write. Now that the British were less of a threat, her work began to change. She began to express concerns about the direction of American politics during the launch of the new Constitution. In 1788, she penned *Observations on the New Constitution,* which was basically a critique.

She stated that the new document contained no Bill of Rights, that there were no limits on the terms of elected leaders, and that there were no protections against the rise of a standing army. Three years later, the Bill of Rights was added.

A History
of the
Revolution

OF THE

RISE, PROGRESS AND TERMINATION

OF THE

AMERICAN REVOLUTION.

INTERSPERSED WITH

Biographical, Political and Moral Obfervations.

IN THREE VOLUMES.

BY MRS. MERCY WARREN,
OF PLYMOUTH, (MASS.)

VOL. I.

BOSTON :
PRINTED BY MANNING AND LORING,
FOR E. LARKIN, No. 47, CORNHILL.
1805.

TITLE PAGE OF HISTORY OF THE RISE, PROGRESS, AND TERMINATION OF THE AMERICAN REVOLUTION (1805)

For more than thirty years, Mercy recorded the details as history took place. Many of the country's greatest leaders corresponded with her and she kept their letters. She wrote a set of books in three volumes containing these historic letters in 1805 called the *History of the Rise, Progress, and Termination of the American Revolution.*

Mercy passed away in 1814 at the age of 86. During her last years she wrote about educational reform and she advocated for women's rights.

JAMES WARREN AND MERCY OTIS WARREN'S GRAVESTONE AND PLAQUE AT BURIAL HILL, PLYMOUTH, MASSACHUSETTS.

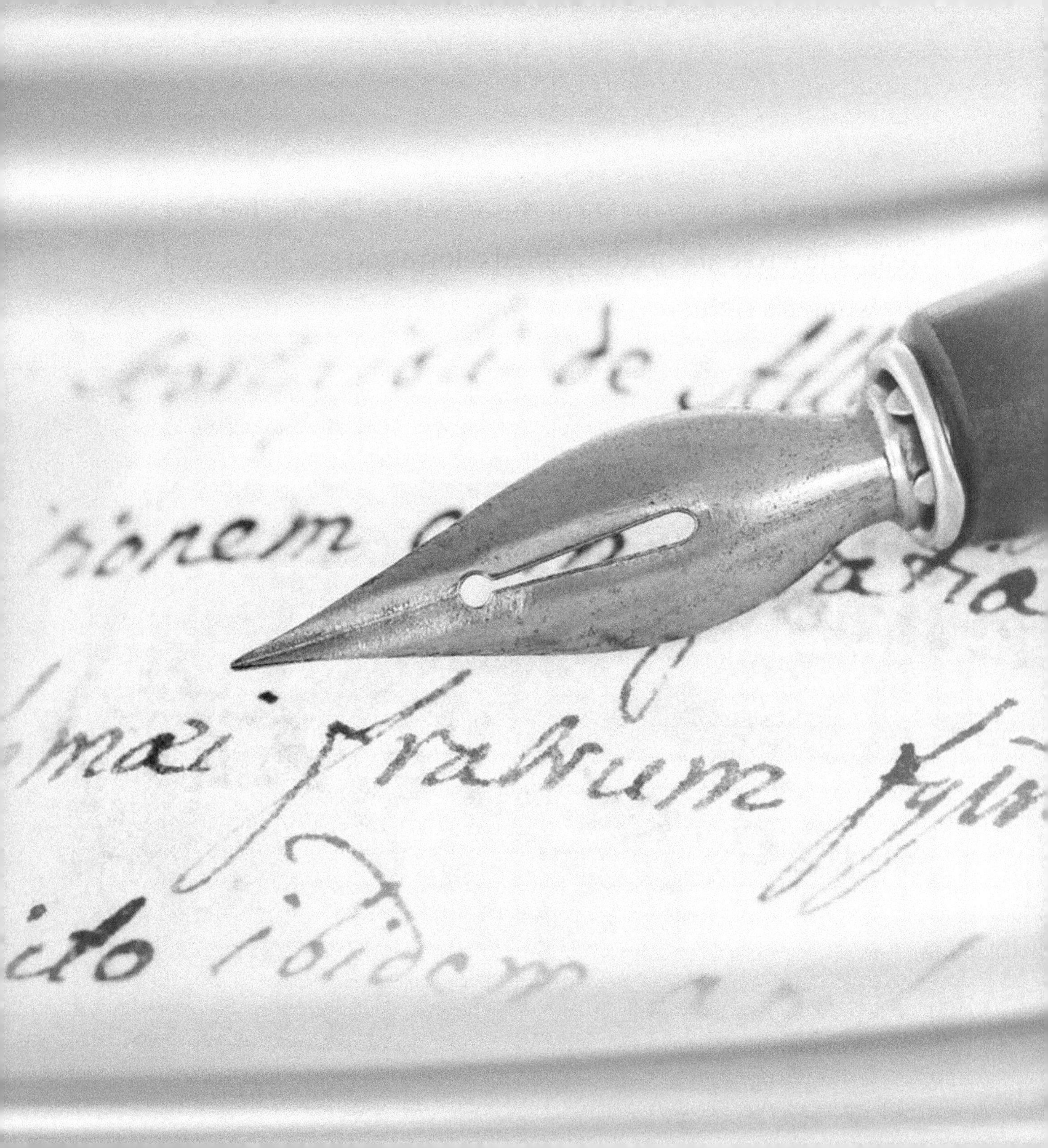

SUMMARY

Mercy Otis Warren was an influential woman writer during the historic period of time prior to and during the American Revolution. At the start, she only wrote for family and friends. Then, she wrote anonymously and eventually she was credited for the work she did to support the cause of the Patriots and the rise of the new nation. Her correspondence with many influential revolutionaries made her history of American independence valuable to a wide audience.

MERCY OTIS WARREN

Awesome! Now that you've learned about Mercy Otis Warren you may want to find out more about the role of women in the American Revolution in the Baby Professor Book, *The Role of Women in the American Revolution - History Picture Books | Children's History Books.*

Visit

www.speedypublishing.com

To view and download free content
on your favorite subject and browse
our catalog of new and exciting
books for readers of all ages.

Lightning Source UK Ltd.
Milton Keynes UK
UKHW051329040121
376379UK00002B/98